fueL presents

INUA ELLAMS'
KNIGHT
WATCH ▶

Written and performed by **Inua Ellams**
Directed by **Thierry Lawson**
Original music by **Zashiki Warashi**

Commissioned by the Albany.
Funded by Arts Council England.
Developed with the support of the Almeida Festival.

the Albany

THEATRE

using public funding by
. S COUNCIL
LOTTERY FUNDED | **ENGLAND**

Inua Ellams

Inua Ellams is a poet, playwright and performer. He has lived in Jos, Plateau State – Nigeria, Dublin – Ireland and London – England, where he currently resides. He has five books published, including his most recent pamphlet of poems *Candy Coated Unicorns and Converse All Stars* (Flipped Eye, 2011).

He also works as a graphic designer/visual artist, as such describes himself as a 'Word & Graphic Artist'. As a workshop facilitator, he has taught in universities, secondary schools, primary schools, theatres, libraries and museums, delivering prose, poetry, occasionally combined with visual art as a stimulus in cross art form workshops. He also delivers workshops through social media networks such as Twitter & Facebook.

His first play *The 14th Tale*, won a Fringe First Award at the Edinburgh Festival Fringe 2009 before touring nationally and transferring to the National Theatre in spring 2010. The show had its international debut at Perth Festival 2012 in February 2012. His second play, *Untitled*, was longlisted for the Alfred Fagon award. It was co-commissioned by Soho Theatre and toured nationally in autumn 2010. His most recent show *Black T-Shirt Collection* was commissioned by Warwick Arts Centre. The show toured nationally in spring 2012 and had a sold out run in the Cottesloe at the National Theatre in April 2012.

Thierry Lawson

Thierry has been a youth theatre director for the past fifteen years. Although mainly being the resident youth productions director at the Tricycle Theatre during that period, Thierry's work has taken him to many various and challenging horizons. Before being offered a place on the Contact Theatre in Manchester's Live and Direct director's course, Thierry travelled the world from his London base working with LIFT, as an Actor with Channel 4 and Discovery in Canada or bringing a taste of Africa to Singapore and Malaysia with Tamtam theatre. More recently Thierry directed Talawa YPT plays and was honoured to be invited to direct *The Last Heroes* by Nick Walker at the Belgrade Theatre Coventry. Thierry likes to brand himself a story teller whether as a film maker: Winner of best short film award for *Block Up* or in theatre where he directed multi-award-winning new writer's project for PUSH 01 at the National Theatre Studio or creating and running the touring education programme for *The Colour of Justice* (Stephen Lawrence inquiry). Thierry directed Inua's previous plays, *The 14th Tale* and *Black T-Shirt Collection*, at the National Theatre and on tour, and *Untitled* at Soho Theatre and on tour.

Zashiki Warashi

The Zashiki Warashi (ZW) drum and flute duo consists of Akinori Fujimoto (drum kit) and Mikey Kirkpatrick (flutes). They have been playing as a duo for five years, with a huge amount of performance experience from the streets and tube tunnels to the Queen Elizabeth Hall in London. They met studying for a music degree at Goldsmiths College. Mikey Kirkpatrick has been playing music since the age of seven, and is now a professional performer, composer, co-producer at Avocado Music Productions, lecturer in composition/performance and curator of the monthly 'Stoke the Fire' event for new music in East London. He also has a solo show called Bird Radio and plays with other ensembles such as The Working Classical Music Orchestra.

Akinori Fujimoto has an MA in Studio Composition from Goldsmiths and a MA in drumming from Tech Music School. As well as teaching in a number of schools, he is involved with a variety of music projects from recording to live shows. He has also toured all over the world with a London-based Japanese Taiko drumming group. Some of the projects he is currently involved with on a regular basis are Chik Budo, Bang Stroke Blow, French for Cartridge and the Boogie Drum School.

The idea for a duo with this instrumentation was inspired by the ancient tradition of bamboo pipe and drum music found across the world – particularly Africa, Asia and Europe. The slave trade carried these sounds to the United States of America and this sonic combination became one of the foundations of the Blues and Jazz that we know well today. The tradition was, until recently, kept very much alive by flautist Otha Turner in Mississippi.

·fueL

Knight Watch is produced by Fuel. Fuel produces fresh work for adventurous people by inspiring artists. Founded in 2004 and led by Louise Blackwell and Kate McGrath, Fuel is a producing organisation working in partnership with some of the most exciting theatre artists in the UK to develop, create and present new work for all.

Fuel is currently producing projects with Will Adamsdale, Belarus Free Theatre, Clod Ensemble, Inua Ellams, Fevered Sleep, David Rosenberg, Sound&Fury, Uninvited Guests and Melanie Wilson. In partnership with higher education organisations, Fuel runs a rolling internship scheme. Our current interns are Kelly Golding from Birkbeck University and Jack Dean from Goldsmiths College. For further information on Fuel, our artists, our team and our internships, please visit www.fueltheatre.com or call 020 7228 6688.

Fuel's recent projects include: *Minsk 2011: A Reply to Kathy Acker* (Belarus Free Theatre); *Electric Hotel* (Requardt & Rosenberg); *Kursk* and *Going Dark* (Sound&Fury); *MUST: The Inside Story* (Peggy Shaw and Clod Ensemble); *Love Letters Straight From Your Heart* and *Make Better Please* (Uninvited Guests); *The Forest* and *On Ageing* (Fevered Sleep); *The 14th Tale* and *Black T-Shirt Collection* (Inua Ellams); *An Anatomie in Four Quarters* (Clod Ensemble) *The Simple Things in Life* (various artists); *Autobiographer* (Melanie Wilson); *The Summer House* (Will Adamsdale, Neil Haigh, Matthew Steer and John Wright).

"One of the most exciting and indispensable producing outfits working in British theatre today."
Guardian

"The maverick producing organisation who are prepared to invest in adventurous artists."
The Herald

Directors **Kate McGrath** & **Louise Blackwell**
Executive Director **Ed Errington**
Producer **Christina Elliot**
Head of Production **Stuart Heyes**
Project Managers **Rosalind Wynn**, **Alice Massey**
(maternity leave) & **Hannah Kerr** (maternity cover)
Technical Coordinator **Billy Wolf**
Administrator **Natalie Dibsdale**

Make Your Mark on Fuel:

At Fuel we are constantly working with artists to create new experiences for you to enjoy. We believe in these aims and work hard every day to make them happen. If you would like to make your mark, visit our website at fueltheatre.com and click on 'support'. There are lots of ways you can get involved. Just £5 a month will help make our ambitions real. In return we'll give you exclusive benefits and the inside story on what we're up to. You'll make great ideas come to life for the broadest possible audience.

You'll keep us going.

To get involved, please download the Make Your Mark form from the Fuel website: www.fueltheatre.com

Thank you from all of us.

A big thank you to our current supporters:

Fuel receives National Portfolio funding from Arts Council England.

With thanks to our catalysts:
Sean Egan, James Mackenzie-Blackman,
Michael Morris, Sarah Preece, Sarah Quelch,
John Tiffany and Nick Williams.

Tour dates

Greenwich+Docklands International Festival
23–24 June
festival.org

International Student Drama Festival, Sheffield
26 June
nsdf.org.uk

Camden People's Theatre
29–30 June
cptheatre.co.uk

Almeida Festival, Spa Fields, Clerkenwell
2–3 July
almeida.co.uk

Tara Theatre @ Coronation Gardens, Southfields
5–7 July
tara-arts.com

Arcola Theatre at the Dalston Eastern Curve Garden
10 July
arcolatheatre.com

The Last Refuge, Peckham
11 July
thelastrefuge.co.uk

Latitude Festival, Southwold Outdoor Theatre Stage
14 July
latitudefestival.co.uk

Southbank Centre, Central London
22 July
southbankcentre.co.uk

Stockton International Riverside Festival
2–3 August
sirf.co.uk

Live Theatre in association with NewcastleGateshead Bridges Festival
4–5 August
live.org.uk

The Albany at Deptford Lounge
21 September
thealbany.org.uk

KNIGHT WATCH

INUA ELLAMS

KNIGHT WATCH

OBERON BOOKS
LONDON

First published in 2012 by Oberon Books Ltd
521 Caledonian Road, London N7 9RH
Tel: +44 (0) 20 7607 3637 / Fax: +44 (0) 20 7607 3629
e-mail: info@oberonbooks.com
www.oberonbooks.com

A catalogue record for this book is available from the British
Library.

PB ISBN: 978-1-84943-404-1
E ISBN: 978-1-84943-555-0

Visit www.oberonbooks.com to read more about all our books
and to buy them. You will also find features, author interviews and
news of any author events, and you can sign up for e-newsletters
so that you're always first to hear about our new releases.

"...from now on cities will be built on one side of the street so that soothsayers will have wilderness to wander and lovers space enough to contemplate a kiss..."

Saul Williams, said the shotgun to the head

All candles are cousins of the sun.
The moon plays foster mother. The waters swear
always to reflect her light. Dust is daughter to these
givers of life, all grandmother'd by nature holding
tight. In this patch-work order, this unclear night,
we all are prodigal sons; we alone journey to spirit
city, but earth remains our home and scattered, we
live across its round dome. We live in wilderness
where vultures coast the sky, where sand storms,
the land is worn, the river beds dry and lush
forests where rain torrents and birds cloud the sky,
where herds stampede past trees, feed on bountiful
evergreens...

But mostly we live in cities where we can't see
stars for fumes, so turn to smashed glass, believing
shards shine like constellations do. We disregard
the sun and the moon who lights us when the dark
looms, instead bow to cement and steel, to stone
pollen and refined minerals that combined, make
mountains that scrape the sky.

In the South East side of one such city lived two tribes, two constant rivals. First was the 'House of Herne' known for bank thievery and slow dealing, for crisp shirts, strict appearances and clipped speech. Slow to anger and slow to forgive, they rose to power in the late Nineties, followed close by the 'Knights of Newtown', the boisterous, brick-built, back street boys, known for loose clothes, deep throats and insults, quick to anger and quick to forgive, they worked in burglaries but ruled the drug deals.

This caused the quarrel. The House wanted the drug market for their own, but The Knights never wished to relinquish the throne. The battles over this were so subscribed to, that almost overnight, after scuffles, graffiti tapestries of fight scenes would be found sprayed on the sprawling urban walls.

I lived amongst The Knights in one tower block, one stone mountain circled by grey mists. I never joined the tribe, so became an outcast, they called me "the young fool" who lived in the past.

I lived alone and for stretches of days the only living things I'd see were trees. And in those days landscaped by stone and steel, those grey mornings and greyer nights, torch-lit by darker thrills, trees were dwindling single things; like me, last rebels from an age long gone, endangered in this city of dust and nylon. If I ever found one, I'd try to help it live. If it died, I'd take it home, wait till it dried and shape into any object I desired. So through me, dead trees would keep living. My first sculptures were small figurines, then palm-sized, then desk-sized and varied in between, but my greatest undertaking was a whole wooden car. It had wooden wheels, wooden tyres, wooden seats, wooden engine, wooden pistons, wooden doors, wooden forks but when I tried it, the car wouldn't work.

Searching for wood one autumn night, I chanced across a disturbance by one small tribe that shattered constellations of glass in bar fights. I was alone and must have seemed like easy prey; the tribe circled me silently, the breeze blew in sympathy. I knew I couldn't run, so though frightened stayed my ground as the nearest one threatened:

"gimme your money, if you don't wanna die"

with a knife in the street light, flashing before my
eyes, I told him all I had was bus fare home. But
this just angered him, his voice grew louder, his
hand shook, he demanded I shut up, advanced
with a dark look. I gave him all I had, dropped
to the ground, covered my face with hands as the
tribe started to punch, kick and spit. The beating
lasted an eternity of minutes then suddenly
stopped. I looked up puzzled to find a fine rain's
drizzle, the tribe's footsteps fizzling into the night
and a hooded figure holding a gun.

"don't shoot, I've got nothing, the tribe took all and ran"
"I don't want money, are you okay?"
"I'm fine, thanks for asking…and…scaring the tribe
away" I said lifting my bundle from where it lay.
"what's that?" she asked
"wood" I replied, she pulled down her hood, I saw the
question in her eyes,
"I turn them into things at my place"
"you're a sculptor" she asked completely disbelieving,
"listen" I said as the rain settled in, "I live a few streets
from here, let's get out of the weather, I'll show you, it's
over there…"

She saved my life, it was the least I could do. Back
at mine, I lit the gas fire and brewed two cups of
coffee, showed her sculptures in the workshop,
intricate figurines, replicas of buildings, door
knockers, wall clocks, the just-started other things;
the half-built model of South East with its tower
blocks like dark fists, threatening into sky.

"you made these?" she asked
"yes" I replied
"show me...I want to learn"
"sorry" I said, my voice level and stern "I don't teach, no
one knows this place is here, I only showed you 'cause
you helped back there"
"I saved your life".
I started to reply, realised she hadn't spoken any lie, if
she hadn't been passing by
I'd be lying on the street,
"okay" I said after minutes of thinking, "but only a few
lessons, and only once a week..."

That night, I agreed to show all I knew about
wood-grain, shaving, joining, sawing, all I'd learnt
from mistakes and books.

For the first month I spoke a lot, she listened.
She'd only interrupt to ask questions with four-
worded sentences – that was patience-testing, like
"please say that again", "pass me the chisel". The
lessons were at night and always interrupted by
the traffic, chatter and laughter wafting in. By the
second month we'd found a rhythm around this.
Then I discovered the danger I was in.

"Call me Lu" she said.

She was older than me, long hair, small nose, deep
dark brows. We talked about land where we could
find wood, grading the areas from bad to good
when she suggested I check the trees fallen by her
place on Croft St,

"where's that?" I asked,
"go past the closed factory, take the first right turn,
through those old fields now covered with fern…,"
"but…that's not safe ground" I said, "that's House of…"
"Herne" she finished.

A shiver travelled the length of my spine. I sat still,
watched her watching me. I made for the door,
she sailed off the table and tackled me to the floor.

"Listen" she said, her hand over my mouth, "I didn't tell
'cause there wasn't need to"
"why now" I screamed through a muffled mouth,
"I didn't mean to" she said, "it slipped out…I let my
guard down…thought we'd become friends"

An awkward silence that never seemed to end, then

"okay" she said, "I'll get off your chest but think carefully
on what you do next"
"This block is owned by The Knights, they hurt people
like you"
"I know" she said, "that's why we work nights",
"but you guys are known as vicious brawlers"
"we are just like you Michael, we go to bed at night"
"but…The Knights won't hear that"
"listen" she said "if you can't handle this, we stop, simple,
but I think you like me and like working this way. If you
wish to continue, pass me a tool, I'll stay, if not, we shake
hands, I'll make my way…"
"damn, that's the most I've heard you say…"

So I pondered on it, looked from her outstretched hand, to the rest of my room, from the four dark corners to all four walls. From the scattered sandpapers, rustling like leaves, to the sheaves of curled shavings under the table. I looked to the ceiling where the light bulb dangling like one small sun swung back and forth and back and forth, I thought about all that could happen, all that could go wrong, shook my head a little...passed her a chisel.

I agreed on one condition, if ever The Knights grew suspicious, I'd end it. No questions, No explanations.

But we never got that far. Unknown to us, our movements were watched by The Knights, they'd kept a steady vigil on us, all the joining and sanding caused a lot of noise and there'd been more of it since Lu joined. By that lesson's end, we had two sacks full of scrap wood to recycle.

We stepped out wearing hoods, carrying one sack each and were instantly surrounded by a tribe of guys in hoods too.

"don't move" one said "we know all about you, trust me
some day you'll join this crew, what are you carrying?"
"just a sack of scrap wood"
"drop it on the ground"
"we're going to the scrap yard, what's this about?"
"just checking things, we like to know what goes in the
hood…who is that beside you?"
"cousin" I lied, my heart beating faster "she's from out of
town"
"let her talk, she seems to know her way around"

I watched in horror as they walked towards Lu,
almost shouted "watch out", I thought they'd catch
her surely, suddenly she lashed out with her leg,
threw the sack at one, uppercut the other, vaulted
their bodies and fled into the night. The one who'd
been speaking screamed in anger, pulled back his
hood and darted after Lu. I caught a glimpse of his
moon-lit face. I'd seen it sprayed on every battle
wall, he was a Knight of Newtown. They called
him Swift.

In all the land of Newtown toughened by steel
and grit, Swift was the fastest, most vicious Knight,
feared for his speed and terrible might, so when
he chased after Lu, I screamed "Hurry! don't stop
for a second!", till the three guys battered me silent
with fists. I stopped struggling after another six
kicks. Swift returned panting heavily. His hands
weren't bloody, so I knew he hadn't caught her.

"Your Cousin? We'll see about that"

Dragged to the street light, Swift held a leather
pouch he opened. I gasped when I saw the card
clasped in his hand. There was a face on it, one
that I knew…

"Lulayan Issac," he spat, "42 Croft St, Herne House. You
hid our enemy, in our own land?!"
"She isn't like…"
"SILENCE! They're laughing at us right now, gotta do
something,
they'll take us for clowns"
"You are wrong…"

I was punched quiet by the men holding me
down. A moment passed then steadily Swift began
to laugh.

"I know…I'll challenge her to a duel."
"No, Swift, don't do that."

A duel is a fight. Two men meet and battle till one
falls, it's an aged tradition, old as stone walls but
these days duels weren't fought with swords but
guns, you fall, you don't get up.

"I'll call her out in front of her tribe, she'll have to answer
for honour and pride."
"What about this one?" the men holding me asked
"Let him go, catch him later, there's nothing he can do"

So Swift sent word through South-East streets, the
duel was set for Wednesday night and I couldn't
sleep, I hadn't heard from Lu. I wanted to believe
she wouldn't take his challenge, but peer pressure
makes us do foolish things, and I was afraid Lu
would fall victim, so I got dressed and crept out
towards the bridge, keeping all the way to the
shadows and side streets.

When I arrived everything was still, even the
traffic seemed to hold its breath, the few trees on
the pavement painted silver by the moon stood
still. No leaf moved. Then under the furthest one,
I saw something glint, saw the sleek design of
cold metal and a similar glimmer from across the
bridge. I ran into the centre, arms out stretched,
fingers splayed as if palms could bounce bullets.
Perched on the white lines, the light turned green,
the cars began flashing towards me. I screamed.
Over the roaring engines:

> "Sorry Lu, Sorry Swift for bringing this between tribes,
> I meant no harm, but bullets won't fix this, put the guns
> down"

but they kept ducking and weaving, trying to shoot
around me. I screamed louder and louder as the
traffic's speed increased,

> "Swift, Lu, bullets won't fix this…"

but they kept ducking…

> "please, listen to me…"

And maybe it was something of the way I spoke,
or the moon bouncing from my chest, or the
dangerous scene of me begging between speeding
cars and light beams, but Lu's forehead cleared,
her frown disappeared, she lowered her gun and
Swift let his anger lift and laughed, his harsh voice
sand-papering past trees into the sky. Then both
of them shouted, arms out stretched, "Michael,
Michael get off the bridge!" I smiled relieved,
wondering who to meet, whose hand to shake first,
Lulayan or Swift, I turned quietly,

into a bus I did not see that charged into me,
knocked me through the ominous sky. Everything
went still. My body, lifted by the force of impact,
flew through the dark, over the rails, smashed the
river flowing below, with blood, like sap, seeping
into water, my skull splintered, my spine snapped.

Lu and Swift ran towards the rails, Swift stood
trembling, Lu choking wails, knowing I could not
have survived the sail, the hundred foot drop, the
churning waves. Swift lifted Lu who'd curled up
like wood shaving, sat her gently on the paving
and called the police.

Both neighbourhoods were quiet that week. In the days after I fell, both tribes gathered to pay respect to me. One minute's silence stretched from The House of Herne and The Knights of Newtown gathered in the cemetery, to solemn tribe members scattered in penitentiaries, who later that night lit a light each, a thousand candle fires linked by wind, blowing to forests and cities in between.

That night, I watched wind lift the leaves,
      wiped one tear from my eye
and stared through fog and rustling rain
      that came when Michael died,
I stared towards the Newtown lands,
      where shadowed towers rise.

The House of Herne and Newtown Knights
      like thugs caked in cotton
had walked the streets in perfect peace;
      for Michael we got on.
We watered flora, planted seeds,
      and pruned what was rotting.

As peace thrived between tribes, they talked
      of new alliances:
Like "KnightsHouse" or "HerneTown" whispered
      into the silences,
but I missed his workshops, his thoughts,
      all of his fantasies

I missed his soft ways, missed my friend
      and missed his furrowed brow.
If I had walked away that night
      he would be alive now.
The peace that reigned came from his death
      I swore to guard it, vowed,

but there were odd things happening.
      I tied my long hair back,
and turned to face the table piled
      with files printed in black;
They told of days when flocks of birds
      exploded from rucksacks.

How once, the bulbs in grey street lamps
      all glowed a greenish blue,
and wild dogs gathered outside, sat
      and howled by Michael's room.
I wondered what these things might mean
      as Cox came running through.

"North of the city off Prime Street
      a Knight too drunk to walk,
knocked one of us straight to the ground.
      so now, the truce is off.
We must avenge, find where he lives…"
      "No Cox", my hand raised up…

"We won't be starting careless wars
          over liquor and lime.
My father left this throne to me
          and I've made up my mind."
"If our men get no revenge
          they'll rise against you, why…"

"If I see fists or one stone thrown
          you'll wake to find me gone."
"You'll go?" Cox asked – his voice now high
          "You'll leave all we have done?
You'll defect? For that…ant who died…"
          I slapped Cox and he sprung.

We clashed mid-air, I scratched him, kicked
          and held him to the floor,
"You know what Cox, do as you wish,
          I won't rule any more,
I stood up, grabbed a hooded shirt
          and crashed through the glass door

as Cox threatened to hunt me down
          to send his hundred spies.
"No place to run, the Knights won't help"
          you've no place left to hide."
Breathless, I ran to Newtown land
          beneath the wind stormed sky.

Two days I hid in alleyways
        as Cox started the war.
Two Knights fell by Herne House knives,
        they fought back fast and raw
till chaos filled the streets again
        and pavements held their blood.

And as the fighters clashed above
        with sticks and stones and guns
I crawled through pipes and sewage drains,
        my hair grew thick with mud.
I surfaced by the corner and
        returned to Michael's shop

where everything was as it was
        even the lone light bulb,
from the scattered sand papers to
        the shelves built on the walls.
I thought of Michael's innocence
        and thought I hear him call.

Then saw my name scrawled on a box.
        I prised off the thin lid,
and found a note in Michael's hand
        addressed to… Lulay… Me?
"If you are reading this my friend,
        something's happened to me.

I don't know what the future holds
        but please go through this box.
And it will bring you peace of mind:
        do as the note instructs.
But Lu, you've got to leave South East
        till then it will not work."

I trembled in his quiet room.
        A soft breeze blew the leaves.
I searched the box, found a reed stick,
        a note, the first line reads…
"To make a simple wooden flute,
        These are the things you need"

Just then a voice: "ANYONE THERE?!
        swear I saw something move!"
They broke the door as I lashed out,
        I grabbed the box and tools,
and crashed through as they chased with dogs
        But I kept on the move.

And while I tunnelled underneath
        such wind storms blew the streets!
And still the strange things happening:
        the night roared with drumbeats
that echoed from dead factories
        that stood on South East Hills.

And still I ran, I only stopped
        to work on Michael's flute.
I'd break into abandoned homes
        to work the stick of wood.
My sweaty clothes choked all my skin
        I never once removed,

for, pressed between my chest and vest
        was Michael's careful note,
he thought he'd die by Swift or I
        yet, took the time and wrote?
Before my worries turned to cries
        I heard Cox getting close.

I ran, I reached the border walls
        and turned to face South East,
Its car fumes rose to kiss the clouds,
        the wind stormed thunderously,
The moon danced through its howling, lit
        the buildings brilliantly.

"But beauty lies in strangest things"
        Michael once said to me.
The flute was almost finished now,
        I'd carved out the mouth piece
and hollowed holes an inch apart,
        and washed the wood with spit

I reached the wall, my fingers raw,
      naked, tore at the stone.
Before I sailed over the top
      a Herne House voice bellowed
"This gun is pointed at your head,
      you betrayed us, your own!"

But just behind, a shadow rose,
      a Knight! I knew his face!
I watched as Swift pulled back his arm
      and pummelled Cox's face.
I lost my balance, falling back
      towards the ground with pace.

And as I fell, the oddest thing,
      a thick wind wrapped me whole,
I knew instinctively to blow,
      pulled out the flute, did so,
and all the rushing air and ground,
      and all of time turned slow

As sound escaped the flute I held
      grey wings grew out its holes
they flapped me gently to the ground
      and shrunk back through the holes.
I noticed the richness of soil
      how well plants here had grown.

I turned as moonlight slipped through clouds
      and licked the giant leaves,
I saw trees tall as stacked street lamps
      branches like tarpaulins
and petals thick as peeling paint
      they slow danced in night breeze.

The grounds rolled into valleys, cliffs,
      real mountains, no grey hills,
and rivers flowed as eyes could see
      did Michael plan all this?
When was he here? Why? How could he?
      Then I heard, loud and shrill

The same noises that left my flute
      they echoed through the dark;
a chorus blown from city slums
      came urgently and sharp
they had called out, they needed help
      and I had to go back.

The new moon rode high crowning the metropolis
shining: a queen on top of us,
and below the dark clouds where gathering
lightning was flashing and forces were amassing and

– battles broke, lives choked inside the battle smoke
and the wicked wind blew hard against our battle cloaks

Gun cocked by the border walls,
I pulled back, struck Cox and he crumpled up,
the boys laughed "stamp down on his broken face"
but I ain't the type to kick a man down in his broken
state.

– Pick him up! March quick through the patchy fields,
that's a direct order son, leave behind the broken hills
– when we reach the city, leave the main streets and
battle fields

rest you guns, shoot only if it's necessary
– detest death, you hear? even among enemies.

But The Knights didn't care, didn't listen to me
I was like a teacher and city was their playing fields.

Tower blocks, I tied Cox to a chair.
Here's a cup of water son, Listen, I don't care.
The battle's out of… shh, tss, Listen!
The battle's out of order, they massacre each other

Out there where the shadows glare,
– where the brittle bones clash and skin tissue tears
where the playgrounds boil and erupt with fear,
there's a dark fire burning, and a reckoning is coming.

Now Cox, I will let you go
if you go tell your men to live life slow
the foolish battle started with a cup of beer,
I gave you cup of water, we can end it here.

Cox spat in my face… "Die Swift,
the city is ours for the taking, as if
you pack of fools were threat to us,
we're gonna flush the city, turn you to dust."

I pulled back, fist clenched, did he do that?
Did I just speak peace? Did he mean to do that?
Is that saliva dripping off my chin?
– I head-butt, head-crush, till he toppled clean,

– a couple men told me Cox was dangerous
once burned a house down 'cause the girl said leave
       saw a man frown, and crushed his knees
       wanted to save the city, and I didn't need this.

(Sound of flutes playing.)

The door was hammered, the men rushed in, "Swift
the House of Herne are taking over Newtown streets
– they're looting the schools, the shops, the banks,
chemists
and setting fire to the alleys, suffocating our men,
I'm telling you when we let scum run free,
when we let them…" shhhs, listen

(Sound of flutes playing.)

"what's that?" they asked. Light flashed.

(Sound of flutes playing.)

Sound like horns, a chorus of flutes
must be hundreds of them, gathered…I'm going to look,
– stay here, watch Cox, he's dumb as he looks
if he stirs, knock him unconscious or give him a book,

That was it, that was me, straight out the door
and I'd never seen South East battered before.
Shattered before, broken and torn, scattered before
with traffic lights rammed through the windows of stores

      pipes burst, water gushing out of it, more
– cars on fire / tyres slashed, windows and doors
– crashed, the glass splintering, lights flickering on.
From the bottom of the street came a riotous roar

      I ducked as rocks flew / over and tore through /
another tribe coming running out of a door.
      Walls crashed, gas flamed into the night,
I tumbled in the street as a tower of smoke roared

into a corner, we washed last week
cleared its rubble planting trees last week. Funny
how little things never mattered before,
but as the little tree fried, I was begging for pause,

I'm telling you, war leaves walls battered and torn
but the true victims, usually: the weak and the poor.

Herne House think that the battle is won,
– but this is South East, I'm Swift, I am the law. Stand UP!
Knee deep in debris, I climbed up.
Had to find the men, had to tell 'em It's Time, STOP!
Had to the find the leaders before my time's up.
Had to find those horns, they make time stop.

Malcolm Street, riddle with heat.
Saw an old lady crying and I gave her some keys
– Take this, a car's parked on Middleton Lane
find your friends, stay together, the city is insane.

Smith Road, was glowing like gold
saw a church like a furnace, burning, splitting the road
– in half, I doubled back, as the thunder clapped
after lightning, the sky turned a darker black.

– Mine Street, hidden by the crumbling church, I saw
many shadows tunnelling through broken stalls,
– some crawled. Each, holding something fragile and small,
a figure by a door waving, beckoning them.

I grabbed from the rubble, thin sticks and I turned
– through the door, up stairs / I followed them up
– flights of stairs, sixth floor, there're twenty of us
– reached the roof, top floor / they're ready to jump.
– they're ready to jump – they're ready to jump –
– they're ready to jump – they're ready to jump –

STOP!

I know the city is on fire,
I know that some nights the smog clogs and makes you tired
foul play rise each month, there's gunfire
and the old folks call it the funeral pyre

– you burn – But the city's got a warmer side
– step from the edge, come, hear about the winter's ride
how stone hills double up as water slides
and in the summer, steel works shine with pride

– don't jump! – don't jump! –

"Don't listen to him, you've seen this before,
        hold the flute, blow through, go tumbling, fall
and wings will lift you to the border walls" –
Said a voice behind me… Lulayan What?!

Didn't I see you fall over a wall?
You're back in the city and you're killing them all.
– "Shut up Swift! I'm not doing this it's Michael"
He died – "Yeah, I'm not sure any more.

– besides, the city is aflame tonight.
and you men, you never know when to fold or fight"

        Lulay snapped her fingers and they turned to dive,
I screamed NO! and stopped when I heard it rise:
        The chorus of horns and the slow of time
– as twenty of them flew through the stormy skies.

(Sound of flutes playing.)

Lulayan Issac, gimme that flute!
"No, it's mine." You must, or I'll take it from you.
"Come on and try" She said, a glint in her eyes
		we tussled and the girl fought wicked and wild

– as the storm grew angry, shook the skies
/ the clouds broke, rain drops hard as ice
– struck our eyes and we turned temporarily blind.

		"Swift stop, there's no need to fight,
let's leave this roof top, its bucketing down
come close, hold my hand, edge of the roof
ready?		I'm blowing the flute…"

(Sound of flutes playing constantly now.)

		We soared over South East
– on the ground, I thought the battle was the wildest.
– But up there, getting lashed by the bullets of rain,
– the wind whipping ridiculous, stars twinkling strange

I saw South East for what it was,
The fires raging, the concrete burned
        walls crumbling, lights flickering off
– and battles scattering right through the slums

from play grounds right to the churches steeped
        courtyards, squares and factories
soot stained and dust scorched, the fire breathed
        and our people crumbled to their knees

every nook, every cranny, every corner, every alley
the flames and the furnace, the rage was tumultuous
– like volcanoes rumbling, it would soon erupt
– like volcanoes rumbling, it would soon erupt.
like a volcano, South East erupts!

I woke up in a forest. The waves must have spat
me outside the city. All I recalled was a flash, my
body lifted off the bridge, the splash, pain, then
nothing. I lay half sunk in water and struggled
to remember my own name. Whatever it was,
something else was strange, I felt different. I threw
up gobs of water. The pebbles and sharp stones
pierced my skin, I gasped and felt the ground
soften beneath! I sneezed, the breeze stilled. I
coughed, the river stopped. I raised a hand, a
drop fell, splashed the still water and rippled along
the bank, tickling the reeds. But I felt it flowing
inside me, through muscle, veins, then pipes,
sewers, drains, I felt the heat of a boiling city,
and South East came flooding back, memories
of Swift, Lulayan, and the bridge. Above, the sky
thundered four times and I sensed the storm's size
coming for South East.

I ran through the forest and saw it once held a
great city. The roots of trees had tangled with
breeze blocks and old iron. Shattered glass had
grown into trees and they glittered like brittle stars
amongst leaf. There were fallen statues dressed
in shrubbery, branches out of windows where
oaks had grown through floorboards and soil had
swallowed houses whole, street after street, block
after block. I closed my eyes and this forest spoke
to me: running river water, hidden streams and
pools. I hiked on till I'd reached the city, a plan
had formed. Lu had to see the forest.

I found a sharp stone, carved a reed flute, chanted
the forest wind through the wood, blew, and
lifted to where Herne House stood, I landed.
Glass shattered and from the shadows, Lu hit the
cobbled stones and dashed past as a man cursed
her, threatening with spies. Whatever needed
doing, I had to do fast.

Lu made for Newtown, I was all she knew so
thought she'd make for my workshop and room. I
arrived first, left notes to build a flute and spent the
days after running the city through as battle broke
between Knights and Herne House.

I gave out boxes and half-built flutes in attics,
basements, crypts, roofs, alleys, even waited in
the gloom for any I thought might help the battles
cool.

The city boiled with smoke and fire and Lulayan
did as I thought she'd do: reached the border
walls, touched the forest floor, saw there was
something worth fighting for and returned to help
those trapped in the city.

I expected her, waited in the fields, hid in the
bushes, begged the wind's calm. As it dropped,
they landed, I walked towards them. Hundreds,
gathered, crouched around Lu, listening as she
talked the happenings through.

"I know you all say the same thing
        all found a box or flute,
all say why we are gathered here
        are mysteries to you.
And though I don't know what to do,
        I know a thing or two."

"The instructions to build the flute
        came from my friend who died."

Lu…

"Just hold a second, young man, now
        the flute means we can glide…"

Lu…it's me, it's Michael.

She turned, screamed, fell down and Swift?!…
helped her to her feet.

"You di…we saw you fall off the bridge.
        Where've you come from?
are you doing this?

  "Lu, I don't know how I'm here, why skies are
  turning or how the flutes work, I just know we
  are wasting time. Our city will fall tonight. A
  storm is coming. Swift, please bring the people
  here, but as you march out set everything to
  burn. Lu, can I lead the tribe of flutes?"

Lu looked at Swift who shrugged and turned from me.

"Michael is your friend, what do you think?"
"Promise you'll be back…" She asked. I nodded and Lu yelled
"They're yours to command, do as you wish."

"Fan out. Go South and West, a quarter to the East, those left come North with me. Climb the border walls, wait for my signal. Swift, I'll watch for you. Right, move quick."

Lu watched as the flute tribe stood beside each other and blew their flutes high. There rose a clamour, a chorus of such force, that all the wind paused, and all the storm sighed and in the brief stillness, we entered the sky.

The storm attacked, thrashed us aside and whipped river water from the wide banks, down the narrow drains, burst the city mains, till South East flooded, never to dry again.

Below, Lu and Swift had gathered both their tribes,
who pushed, bullied, till all the folks had climbed
the hills of South East, and turned to watch the
tide drown the flaming city, never to burn again.

Block after block, shook at their base, shuddered
as wet soil sucked in trains, swallowed whole
streets; such was the damage, roads couldn't be
built again.

And as fires struggled, as water drowned, as earth
sucked the city, I called the wind down, I gave up
my breath, took the tempest in, called the flute
tribe, "Now, together blow" and all the sounds
united, through the great storm struck the high
towers, turned them to low plains so the city's
stench, would never blow again.

We watched spires twist, heard fires hiss, saw
bridge after road after courtyard all sink.
Newspapers, boxes, clothes, sheets, bowls and
islands of waste dipped below. The last roof beam
slipped beneath the water. The city was destroyed,
utterly and grim.

I collapsed, I fell. I recall the rush of air, but woke on the ground where a fight had begun.

"Behind you", I shouted. "There's a forest filled with homes, they're old but there're houses, grown into trees, ask Lulayan Issac, she knows what I have seen. Lu nodded swiftly, "Over the wall, you'll see…"

And all the people gathered on South East's hills turned towards the borders, lost, confused but free, eyes blazing like candles lit.

And all candles are cousins of the sun. The moon plays foster mother. The waters swear always to refelct her light. Dust is daughter to these givers of life, all grandmother'd by nature holding tight, in this patch-work order, this unclear night, we all are prodigal sons. We alone journey to spirit city, but earth remains our home.

WWW.OBERONBOOKS.COM